SO-CPQ-946

Strings Around the World

by Joanna Solins
illustrated by Ken Stetz

Harcourt

Orlando   Boston   Dallas   Chicago   San Diego

Visit *The Learning Site!*

www.harcourtschool.com

Stringed instruments are used to play all kinds of music. They come in many forms, shapes, and sizes. Whether they are played solo, with an accompanist, or in a band, these instruments make music that people love to hear.

Although they may look easy, most stringed instruments are difficult to play well. To master many of them, you have to practice for years. If you've ever listened to someone who is just starting out on the violin, you may have grimaced at the sound. Yet a good violinist can use the same instrument to make beautiful music.

How does a string make sounds?

When a string is stretched tight, it can be made to vibrate by plucking or drawing a bow across it. These vibrations in the string cause the air to move in waves. When the waves reach our ears, we hear them as sound. The sound created by a string alone is not very loud. You can make the sound louder by attaching the string to a resonator. A *resonator* is a hollow container that picks up the vibrations of the strings and makes the sound louder.

Pitch is how high or how low sound is. Long, loose, thick strings make lower sounds. Short, tight, thin strings make higher sounds. Often, you can change the note a string creates by pressing the string down to make it shorter.

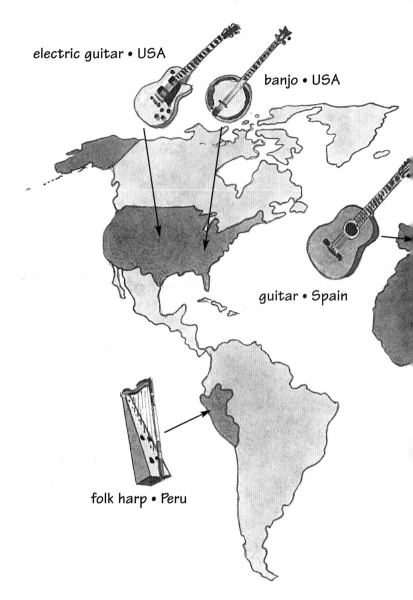

electric guitar • USA

banjo • USA

guitar • Spain

folk harp • Peru

This map shows where many stringed instruments came from. In the past, these instruments may have been used in only one place. Now, many are used all over the world.

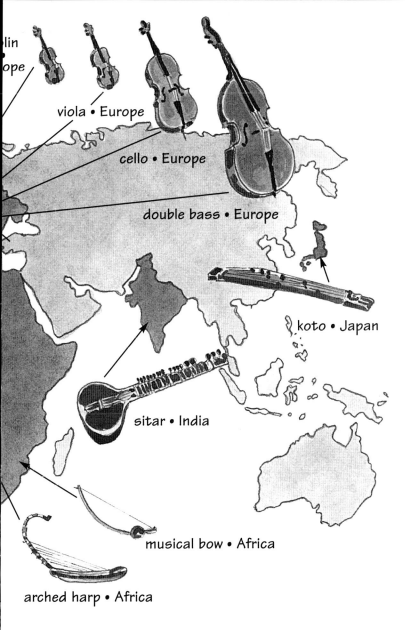

lin
ope

viola • Europe

cello • Europe

double bass • Europe

koto • Japan

sitar • India

musical bow • Africa

arched harp • Africa

Stringed Instruments from Africa

The Musical Bow A musical bow is made from a string stretched between the two ends of a stick. It looks like an archer's bow. It can be played by plucking the string, tapping it with a stick, or rubbing it with a smaller bow. Bows of different sizes can be attached to each other to form one instrument in which each string plays a different note. Adding a resonator makes the sound louder. Anything hollow can act as a resonator.

The Arched Harp The arched harp is one of the most common forms of the harp. It's probably the oldest, too. There are many kinds of arched harps. Most have a bow-shaped neck. Strings are stretched between the neck and the body. Because the instrument is curved, the strings have different lengths and different pitches. People played these instruments in Egypt over 5,000 years ago. They are still being played in many parts of Africa today.

Stringed Instruments from Europe

The Guitar The modern classical guitar was designed by a man from Spain in the 1800s. He put together parts of earlier guitars to form the six-stringed guitar that is still played today. The guitar has a large body with a flat front and back, separated by curving side pieces. The neck has a fingerboard with metal *frets*.

Classical guitars have strings made of animal gut or nylon. Folk guitars are a lot like classical guitars but often have strings made of steel. Guitar strings are played by plucking and strumming.

The Violin Family The violin family has four members—the violin, the viola, the cello, and the double bass. These instruments have similar shapes and sounds, but they have different sizes. They all have a large resonating body and a thin neck.

They all have four strings that run over a high *bridge* on the lower part of the body.

> A **bridge** lifts the strings off the body of the instrument.

These instruments are usually played with a bow. They can also be plucked. This method is called "pizzicato." The shape of the bridge allows the player to sound just one string at a time or to play two or more strings simultaneously. The pitch is changed by pressing the strings down on the neck to change their length.

The violin is the smallest, highest member of the family. It is used to play all kinds of music. The viola looks like a large violin, but it has a lower, darker tone.

The cello is far too big to be held on the shoulder like a violin or a viola. Instead, it rests between the musician's knees. The cello has a warm tone. It can cover a wider range of notes than any other member of the family.

The double bass is the largest member of the violin family. It is over six feet tall. The musician stands or sits on a high stool to play it. The double bass is found in orchestras and is also used in jazz bands.

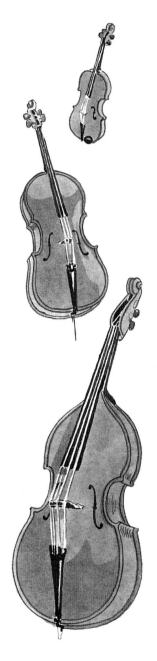

Stringed Instruments from Asia

The Koto The koto is the national instrument of Japan. It has thirteen silk strings. Each string has its own movable bridge. The koto is so long that it must rest on the floor when played. The musician plucks the strings with the thumb and the first two fingers of the right hand, often using three *plectra*. With the left hand, the musician presses down on the other side of the bridge to change the pitch of the strings. The koto is used for instrumental music or as an accompaniment for singing and dancing.

A **plectrum** (plural **plectra**) is often used to pluck strings. Plectra come in many shapes. The most common have a pointed end to pluck the strings and a rounded end to hold. Guitar picks are a type of plectrum.

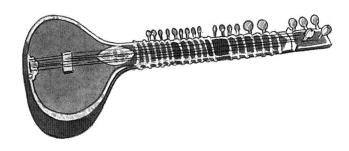

The Sitar The sitar is very popular in northern India. It has a very long neck. The arrangement of strings is very complicated. Several main strings pass over a bridge on the body and over the frets on the neck. These strings, played with a wire plectrum, are used for the melody. The sitar also has other strings called "drone strings." They make a low sound under the melody. It also has strings called "sympathetic strings." They run underneath the frets on the neck. Each of these strings is tuned to a different pitch.

All these different strings can make the sitar sound as if two or three instruments are being played at once! The sitar became well known to rock and roll fans in the 1960s. The Beatles used it in several of their hit songs.

Stringed Instruments from America

The Banjo The banjo developed from African instruments that were brought to America during the 1700s. A banjo has a long neck with frets and a round body. It has anywhere from four to nine strings. It is played by plucking the strings with the tips of your fingers. In the early 1900s, the banjo was played in many jazz bands. Now, it is used mostly to play folk music.

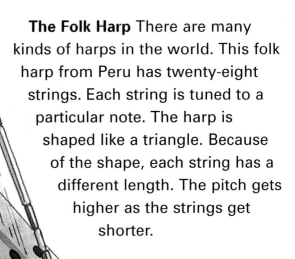

The Folk Harp There are many kinds of harps in the world. This folk harp from Peru has twenty-eight strings. Each string is tuned to a particular note. The harp is shaped like a triangle. Because of the shape, each string has a different length. The pitch gets higher as the strings get shorter.

Electric Guitar The electric guitar is shaped and played very much like a classical guitar. However, it has a solid body instead of a hollow resonating one. In order to make sound, the vibrations of the strings are changed into electrical signals. These signals are sent to an amplifier, which changes them back into sound. A loudspeaker makes the sound louder. The electric guitar was developed in the 1930s and 40s. It is often used in rock and popular music.

String Master Yo-Yo Ma

Yo-Yo Ma is one of the finest cellists in the world. He is so well known and admired that he does not have to audition, as most musicians do. Instead, he is invited to play with orchestras all over the world. In addition to performing live, Ma has done many recording projects. He also likes to help young musicians. He has even

appeared on *Sesame Street* and *Mr. Rogers' Neighborhood*. Ma is very interested in linking traditional music with modern music. He also likes to explore new ways to use his instrument and to experiment with technology. Above all, Yo-Yo Ma loves to share his love of music with people of all ages.

Yo-Yo Ma was born in Paris in 1955. His parents, both Chinese, were also musicians. He began playing the cello when he was four years old and had his first concert when only five. His family moved to New York when he was seven. As a teenager, he studied music at the Juilliard School. Although he was already a famous musician, Ma decided not to major in music when he was at Harvard University. Instead, he majored in anthropology. This subject looks at people all over the world. He was interested in learning how different cultures have shared ideas throughout history.

Yo-Yo Ma thinks the cello is an excellent way to express himself. He says he loves the cello because it has "the exact range of the human voice." He says this makes it "a very human instrument."

Although the cello is usually viewed as a classical instrument, Ma has not limited his playing to sonatas and symphonies.

Ma has done many projects with other musicians, including a recording of Appalachian folk music and one with well-known singer Bobby McFerrin. Ma has also made one cello sound like sixty by connecting it to a computer. When it comes to making music, Yo-Yo Ma enjoys trying just about anything!

Make Your Own Stringed Instrument

Now that you have learned how strings make music, you can make your own sounds with strings. Try using rubber bands, fishing line, thin wire, or any kind of string you can find around the house or in the classroom. For a resonator, you can use empty boxes, milk cartons, soda bottles, tin cans, or other hollow objects.

Experiment with different lengths and kinds of string. What happens when you pull the strings tight? What happens when you leave them loose? What happens when you put the same kinds of strings on different kinds of resonators? Use your imagination. The possibilities are endless!

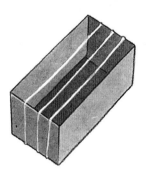